An Introduction to Web Page Design

Christopher Lampton

A First Book

Franklin Watts
A DIVISION OF GROLIER PUBLISHING

NEW YORK   LONDON   HONG KONG   SYDNEY
DANBURY, CONNECTICUT

Note to Readers: Terms defined in the glossary are *italicized* in the text.

Photographs ©: The Children's Museum of Indianapolis, 1996: 7; David Strass: 53; NASA: 44, 56; Smithsonian Institution, 1996: 14.

Library of Congress Cataloging-in-Publication Data

Lampton, Christopher.
    Home page : an introduction to Web page design / by Christopher Lampton.
        p. cm. — (A First book)
    Includes bibliographical references and index.
    ISBN 0-531-20255-0 (lib.bdg.)   0-531-15854-3 (pbk.)
       1. HTML (Document markup language)—Juvenile literature. 2. Web sites—
Juvenile literature. [HTML (Document markup language)] I. Title. II. Series.
QA76.76.H94L34   1997
005.7'2—dc20   96-41130
                                                       CIP

Contents

Preface

The World Wide Web is one of the most exciting parts of the international computer network called the *Internet*. It's made up of millions of electronic documents called *Web pages*, which can be viewed using a computer program called a *Web browser* on any computer connected to the Internet. These Web pages feature words, pictures, animated cartoons, sounds, and even computer programs. Most importantly, Web pages contain special words and pictures, called *hyperlinks*, that let you jump to other places on the Web.

If you've visited the Web, then you already know this. (And if you don't, you might want to pick up a copy of my book *The World Wide Web*, also published by Franklin Watts.)

In this book, you're going to go beyond browsing the Web. I'll show you how to become part of the Web yourself by creating your own Web page!

You may think this requires sophisticated software and a lot of special knowledge, but it doesn't really. In the pages that follow, you'll learn how to create an impressive Web page of your own, using only an ordinary computer and a *text editor*, both of which you may already own. If not, you may be able to get access to them at your school or library.

Once you learn how to create your own Web page, you'll be able to express yourself to millions of people worldwide. You'll probably be surprised by how easy it is.

Anatomy of a Web Page

When you boot up your browser and enter the Web, you can view millions of Web pages made up of fancy typefaces (such as **bold** or *italic*), colorful pictures, clever animation, and interesting sounds. Perhaps you've wondered what goes on behind the scenes to make this possible. For all the flashy graphics and sounds, the foundation of a page on the World Wide Web is a relatively simple *data file* filled with words.

All the information stored on your computer is arranged in data files. These files can contain just about any kind of information, from computer programs to words to pictures. The data files are recorded on the surface of a disk, which may be a portable diskette or the permanent *hard drive* inside your computer, where they can be retrieved whenever you need them.

As I mentioned before, Web pages are made up of data files containing only words (and usually a few numbers and symbols). Because these are simple *text files,* you can create them on your computer using only a text editor.

It may sound hard to believe, but you can create your own pages on the World Wide Web just by typing words. That's what this book is about. By the time you've finished reading this book, you'll be able to create Web pages of your

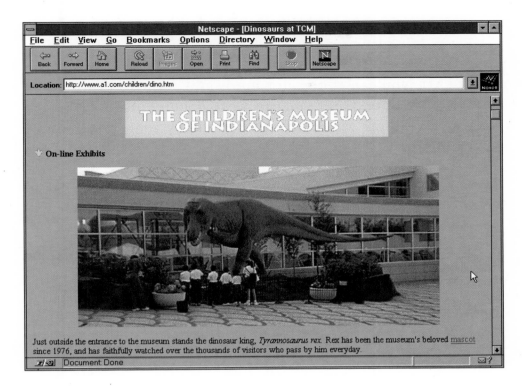

Web pages, such as this one at the Children's Museum of Indianapolis, can be filled with pictures, sounds, and even animation.

own. The only equipment you'll need is a computer—at home, at school, or at your local library—and a couple of computer programs, which we'll discuss later.

HYPERTEXT MARKUP LANGUAGE

To make your own Web page, you'll also need to learn *HyperText Markup Language* or *HTML* for short. HTML is a way of writing text so that it can contain different type-faces, special formatting, and even pictures. In fact, with HTML you can even put sounds and animated cartoons in a page of text. Yet you can write documents in HTML using a simple text editor that probably came with your computer.

All Web pages are written in HTML. To see what an HTML document looks like with its special typefaces and pictures, you need to look at it using a Web browser. One of the most popular browsers around is called Netscape Navi-gator, and this is the one we will use to show the examples in this book.

AN HTML EXAMPLE

Here's a look at an HTML document as it might appear when you create it in a text editor:

```
<html>
<head>
<title>A Demonstration Web Page</title>
</head>

<body>
<h1>Creating Your Own Web Page</h1>
<p>This book is about writing your own Web pages
using HTML notation.You can learn more about this
subject at our <a href="page2.htm">second web
page</a>.</p> <img src="picture.jpg">
```

```
</body>
</html>
```

This HTML document may not look very interesting now, but if you were to look at it with a Web browser, you'd see something that looks a lot more like a page on the World Wide Web. Figure 1 shows how this page would look when viewed with the Netscape browser. Suddenly, there is a picture on the page! The text is in different typefaces and sizes and is neatly formatted. In fact, behind every page on the

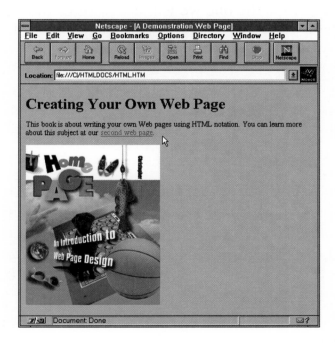

Figure 1

World Wide Web is an HTML document such as this one. Throughout this book, when we refer to a page in its uninterpreted HTML form, we'll call it an HTML document. When we refer to a page as it is seen through a Web browser, we'll call it a Web page.

A QUICK TOUR OF HTML

In the next chapter, we'll show you how to type an HTML document yourself and view it using a Web browser. In later chapters, we'll show you some features you can use to make your page more sophisticated.

For now, though, we'll just take a quick look at the various parts of the page we just created and see what makes it tick. If you don't understand all of this right away, don't worry. We'll spend the rest of this book showing you how to do the things we've done on this page, plus some additional tricks that will come in handy for creating Web pages of your own.

HTML TAGS

First off, you'll notice that the original HTML document is filled with words inside < and > marks. These symbols are sometimes called angle brackets. In HTML, a letter or word surrounded by angle brackets is called a *tag*. We'll have a lot more to say about HTML tags in Chapter Three. For now, we'll just say that they are the way we tell a Web browser how we want our page to appear on the computer screen.

Tags usually come in pairs, with the second tag of the pair beginning with a slash symbol (/). For instance, you'll notice that our HTML document begins with the tag <html> and ends with the tag </html>. The first tells the Web browser that we are beginning a page of information written in HTML notation. The second tells it that the page is over.

After the opening <html> tag, you'll see a tag that reads <head>. This tells the browser that we're going to give it some *header* information, which will tell it important things about the HTML document that is to follow. The header information is what we've put between the <head> tag and the </head> tag.

The only header information we've given the browser is the title of our page, which we've placed between the <title> and </title> tags. The title of this page is "A Demonstration Web Page." If you look at Figure 1, you'll notice that this title doesn't even appear on the Web page. Rather, it appears on the top bar of the Web browser's window.

THE <body> OF THE PAGE

Now that we've gotten the header out of the way, we can jump into the *body* of the document. The body of an HTML document is the part where we describe what the main part of the Web page will look like. If you've looked carefully at the example, you've probably guessed that the body of the document begins with the <body> tag and ends with the </body> tag.

Anything that gets typed between these two tags that isn't in angle brackets will appear on the Web page as text. For instance, if all you typed between the <body> and </body> tags was—This is my first Web page—then that's

title

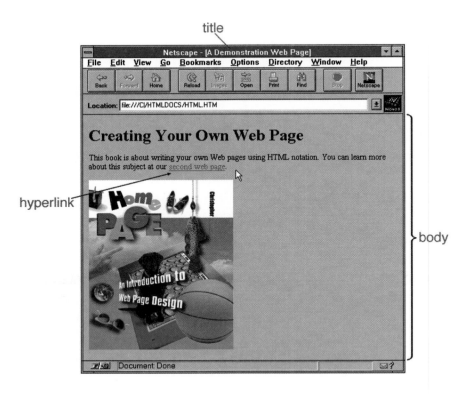

hyperlink

body

This is our demonstration Web page with
the title, body, and hyperlink labeled.

all that would appear on your page. However, there are a lot
of additional tags we can use to show the Web browser how
to display this text or to add features such as pictures.

In the example above, we start the body of the page with
a *heading* (not to be confused with the "header" information
that comes between the <head> and </head> tags). This
heading is the text that goes between the <h1> and </h1>
tags. (There are other numbers that can follow the "h" in
the header tag, as we'll see in Chapter Three.) The heading

tags tell the browser to display this text in extra large letters, so it will stand out from the rest of the page. The heading that we've used reads "Creating Your Own Web Page."

The text that follows the heading appears between the *paragraph tags* <p> and </p>. These tell the browser to start this text at the beginning of a new line on the page, like a paragraph in a book. In a typical HTML document, most of the text will appear between these two tags.

ANCHORS AWEIGH!

You may have noticed additional tags between the paragraph tags. These tags mark an *anchor* in the text. An anchor begins with the <a> tag and ends with the </a> tag, but you'll notice that there's more to the <a> tag than that. In this case, it also contains the term "href" and an equals sign (=) followed by the name of a computer file (**page2.htm**). Don't panic if this is confusing. We'll talk more about it later.

When viewed with a Web browser, this anchor appears as a hypertext link, or hyperlink. This means that the text between the <a> and </a> tags is displayed in a color different from the rest of the text and is usually underlined. And if you click on this text with your mouse pointer, you'll be taken somewhere else on the Web. In our example, clicking on the hyperlink will take you to another Web page named **page2.htm**. The filename in the <a> tag tells the Web browser where it's supposed to take you. We'll show you examples of this in Chapter Four, so don't worry if it doesn't make sense right away.

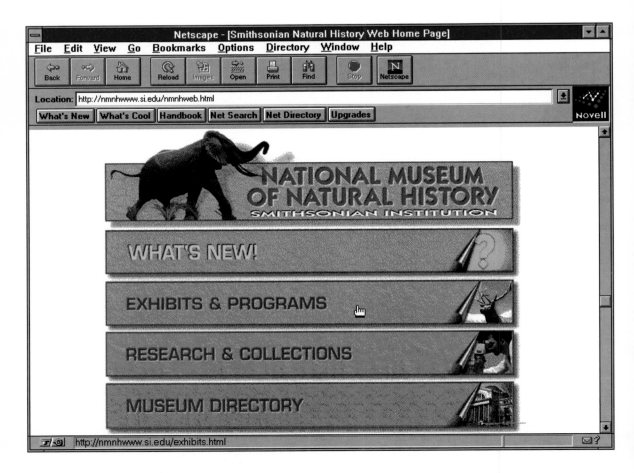

Pictures are an important part of Web pages. The pictures in this Web page by the Smithsonian Institution's National Museum of Natural History make it much more appealing.

ADDING PICTURES

Perhaps the most exciting things we can do with HTML is add pictures to our Web page. We've added a picture to our demonstration page with the <img src="picture.jpg"> tag, called an *image tag*. This tag tells the browser where it can find a picture file, in this case named **picture.jpg**, that can be displayed along with the text on the page. This tag does not need to be closed, so you'll notice that there is no </img src> tag to go with the first (and only) image tag.

In Chapter Four, we'll show you how this works. We'll even talk about how to create your own pictures to put on the World Wide Web.

AND AWAY WE GO

At this point, you're probably itching to learn how to write HTML documents of your own. Before we can talk further about HTML, though, we'll have to talk about the tools you'll need for creating and viewing your own Web pages. You may already have access to these tools and not know it, so that's the subject of our next chapter.

Building a Web Page

CHAPTER TWO

Aside from a knowledge of HTML, you need only two things in order to create a Web page: a text editor and a Web browser. Neither of these programs should be very hard to find. Surprisingly, you don't need a connection to the World Wide Web, though you'll eventually want one if you plan for other people around the world to be able to look at your page, too.

This is what our example HTML document looks like in Notepad, a text editor that comes with Windows 3.1.

TEXT EDITORS

A text editor is a program that lets you type text—that is, words, numbers, and symbols. You may already use a text editor to type your homework or letters to friends. A powerful text editor with lots of features is called a word processor. It's not recommended that you use a word processor, such as Microsoft Word or WordPerfect, to type your HTML documents. These programs sometimes put codes in the text that a Web browser can't understand, and they don't always save your file in such a way that a Web browser can easily find it.

A simple text editor is the best thing to use. Fortunately, you probably already have one of these, even if you don't know it. For instance, if you use the Windows operating system, then you should have a text editor called Notepad, Write, or WordPad somewhere on your hard disk. (If you can't find these files, ask somebody who knows about your computer if they can install these files for you from the original Windows disks.) If you use a Macintosh, you should have a text editor called SimpleText.

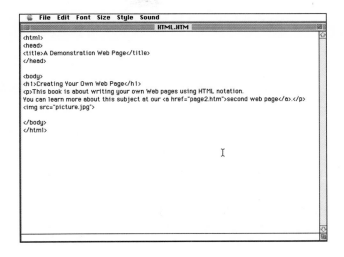

This is our example HTML document again, this time in SimpleText, a text editor that comes with Macintosh computers.

YOUR FIRST WEB PAGE

Once you've found a good text editor, all you have to do is run it and start typing. For instance, try typing the following:

```
<html>
<head>
<title>My First Web Page</title>
</head>

<body>

<h1>This is an HTML Heading</h1>

<p>Anything that I type in the body of this page that
isn't between angle brackets will become part of my
first Web page!</p>

</body>
</html>
```

You can now stop typing. Congratulations! You've created your first Web page!

Save this file to your hard disk under the name **webpage1.htm**. (The htm at the end of the name indicates that it contains HTML information. If you are using a Macintosh or Windows 95, which can handle longer filenames, you can name your page **webpage1.html**.) Be sure to remember where on your disk you saved it. If you don't know how to save a file using your text editor, click on the Help menu and look for instructions on file saving.

Next, you'd probably like to see how this page would appear if it were on the World Wide Web. To do that, you'll need a Web browser.

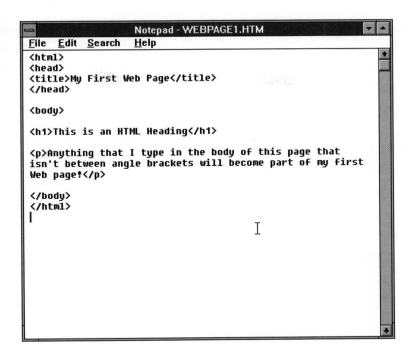

This is **webpage1.htm** shown using Notepad.

WEB BROWSERS

A Web browser is the program you use to view pages on the World Wide Web. Basically, it's a program that translates files written in HTML into neatly formatted text with pictures on your computer screen. If you've been on the World Wide Web before, then you've used a Web browser. However, you may not be aware that you can also use a Web browser to view HTML documents on your own hard disk. That's why you can develop a Web page without being connected to the Web. We'll talk more about that in a minute.

At the time this book was written, the most popular Web browsers were Netscape Navigator and Microsoft Internet Explorer. The Web pages that we create in this book will look fine on either of these browsers. If you don't already have a copy of one of these programs, you can probably get one or the other for free. The company that provides you with access to the Internet may give you a copy of one of these programs if you ask. If you're using a computer at your school to create your Web page, check to see if there's a copy of one of these programs somewhere on the hard disk. If you

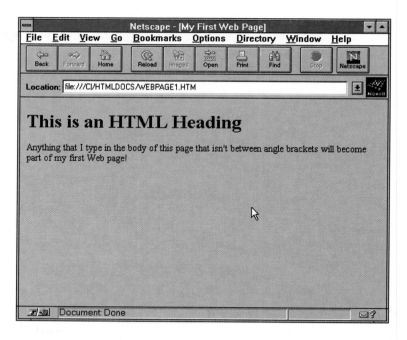

Figure 2

have a friend who's already on the World Wide Web, he or she may be able to *download* a copy of these programs for you. Both companies have been known to give away their browsers freely over the Web, though in some cases you may be expected to pay for them at a later date.

Once you have a Web browser, you can easily use it to look at the Web page you created with your text editor. Run the browser and pull down the File menu in the upper left-hand corner of the screen. If you're using Netscape, you'll see an item marked Open File. Click on this item with your mouse pointer and a dialog box will pop up; use your mouse to select the file you created with the text editor or type the filename in directly. If you type the name, be sure to type the full name, including the name of the disk drive and any subdirectories you may have stored the file in. Then press Enter and—presto!—the Web page should appear on the screen.

Figure 2 shows what the Web page we created above looks like when viewed using Netscape. You should see something similar using your own Web browser.

MULTITASKING

To develop a Web page, you'll need to run your text editor and your Web browser at the same time. Fortunately, both the Windows and Macintosh operating systems are capable of multitasking—that is, running more than one program at once. So it shouldn't be hard to boot up your text editor, then boot up your Web browser, and switch back and forth between the two.

When multitasking, you can type or make changes to an HTML document in your text editor, save the changes, then switch your Web browser to view the page. Most Web browsers will require you to select a menu item called either Reload or Refresh before you can see any changes you've made to your page. The changes won't appear automatically.

Now that you've set up both a Web browser and a text editor, you're prepared to follow along with the HTML examples that we'll see in the following chapters. And then you'll be ready to create Web pages of your own!

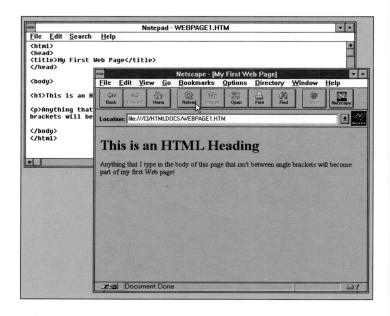

Both the Windows and Macintosh operating systems allow you to keep your text editor and Web browser open at the same time.

HTML Tags

CHAPTER THREE

Tags are the building blocks of HTML. As you saw in Chapter One, tags tell the Web browser how to display the Web page on a computer screen. At their simplest, tags merely tell the Web browser to start a new paragraph or print a line of text in very large letters. At their most complicated, tags can display a picture or create a hyperlink between two Web pages. Tags can even be used to start a computer program running in the middle of your Web page, though that's a subject we won't have room to talk about in this book.

A tag is simply a letter, word, number, or combination of these placed between angle brackets—the < and > symbols. Every tag represents an HTML feature. Most tags come in pairs, the first of which turns the feature on, the second of which turns the feature off. The second tag—the one that turns it off—usually looks like the first tag with a slash symbol (/) in front of it. For instance, the <p> and </p> tags tell the browser where a paragraph begins and ends.

THE SIMPLEST HTML DOCUMENT

The most basic tags in your HTML document tell the browser that the document is written in HTML, give it the header information, and show it where the body of the document is described. Thus, the simplest possible HTML document would look like this:

```
<html>
<head>
</head>
<body>
</body>
</html>
```

Of course, if you were to type this HTML document with your text editor and look at it with your Web browser, you wouldn't see anything because it translates into a completely blank Web page. There wouldn't even be a title on your browser's top line (though your browser may display the name of the HTML file there instead). Still, it is a completely valid Web page, and your browser should have no objection to displaying it, invisible though it is.

THE <html> TAG

As we mentioned in the first chapter, the <html> tag tells the browser that an HTML document is starting, and the </html> tag tells it that the document has ended. These are the most basic HTML tags. In general, everything else in your document should come between these tags.

THE <head> AND <title> TAGS

After the <html> tag but before the body of the document, you'll need to put a header. The header of an HTML doc-

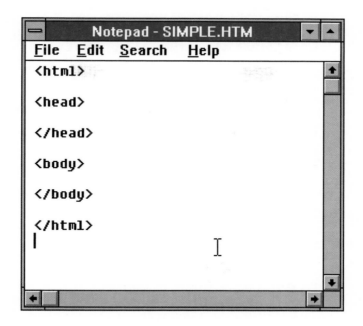

The simplest HTML document

ument always begins with the <head> tag and ends with the </head> tag. You can put several things between these tags, but for most HTML documents all you'll need is a title. This specifies the title that goes on the top bar of the Web browser's window when it's displaying your page. The title begins with the <title> tag and ends with the </title> tag, like this:

<title>This Is the Title of My Page</title>

Remember that the title should come after the <head> tag but before the </head> tag.

THE <body> TAG

The <body> tag shows where the real action is in an HTML document. Between the <body> and </body> tags comes everything the browser will display on your Web page. This is where you'll put text, pictures, hyperlinks—and anything else you may want on your page.

Any text you type between these two tags that doesn't have angle brackets around it will appear directly on your page. For instance, if the body of your HTML document looks like this:

<body>This is it!</body>

then your entire Web page will consist of the words "This is it!"

You can use additional tags in the body of the document to tell the Web browser how to display the text of your page. We'll talk about several of these tags later in this chapter.

HTML COMMENTS

Suppose you want to write something in your HTML document that you don't want to appear in your Web page. You can do this with the *comment tag*. The tag that turns the comment on is <!-- and the tag that turns the comment off is -->. These tags tell the browser to ignore anything that comes between them. For instance, if you put this line in your HTML document:

<!-- This is just a comment -->

it wouldn't cause the browser to display anything at all. The words "This is just a comment" would not appear anywhere in your Web page.

Why would you write something the browser would ignore completely? An HTML comment is a kind of note you write to yourself or anyone else who might read the uninterpreted HTML document. You can put comments anywhere in the document; think of them as being like the notes you write in the margins of a schoolbook to remind yourself of important stuff. But keep in mind that other people will be able to view the HTML document for your Web page (this is called viewing the *source*), so don't write anything you wouldn't want other people to see. We'll talk more about viewing the source of Web pages later.

AN HTML TEMPLATE

Here's an example of how you might use HTML comments. Remember the simplest possible HTML document we saw earlier in this chapter? Here it is again, with comments added:

```
<!-- This is a template for a simple Web page written
in HTML -->

<html>
<head>

<!-- This is where you put the title for your page -->
```

```
<title>This is my page</title>

</head>

<body>

<!-- This is where you place the text that you want to

appear on your Web page. -->

</body>

</html>
```

Here's an important tip: type this page using your text editor and save it to your disk under the name **template.htm**. Then, when you want to create a new Web page, just load this page into your text editor and use the Save As command to save it as a second file, with a name such as **mypage.htm**. You can then add the text for your new page to this new file and save it again. That way, you won't have to keep typing these basic tags every time you design a new Web page. This kind of file is called a *template*.

You're now ready to create the body of an HTML document. This is your chance to be creative. In the next few sections, we'll talk about the tags you'll use to format your text (that is, make sure it's laid out the way you want it to be).

THE <p>ARAGRAPH TAG

Most Web pages are broken into paragraphs. However, you can't just type paragraphs with your text editor and expect the Web browser to know how to display them, because it will ignore

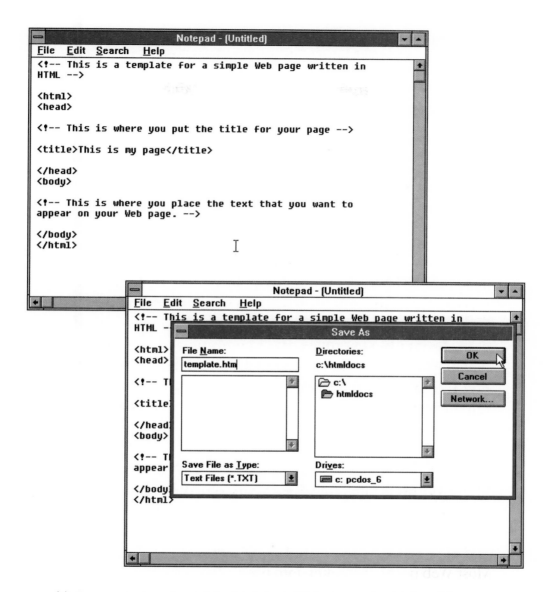

You can create a template for future Web pages by typing this text into your text editor (top) and saving it as **template.htm** (bottom).

carriage returns or extra lines in your text. For instance, suppose you typed this text in the body of the template we just created:

```
<body>

Four score and seven years ago, our forefathers
brought forth upon this continent a new nation,
conceived in liberty and dedicated to the proposition
that all men are created equal.

To be or not to be, that is the question.

</body>
```

Your new HTML document would look like figure 3. If you viewed this with your browser, you might expect that you'd have two paragraphs of text on your Web page. This is not the case. In fact, your browser will combine the two into one paragraph, as in figure 4. That's why you need the paragraph tag. In HTML, each paragraph of text begins with the <p> tag and ends with the </p> tag. Here's the previous body text rewritten with the paragraph tag:

```
<body>

<p>Four score and seven years ago, our forefathers
brought forth upon this continent a new nation,
conceived in liberty and dedicated to the proposition
that all men are created equal.</p>

<p>To be or not to be, that is the question.</p>

</body>
```

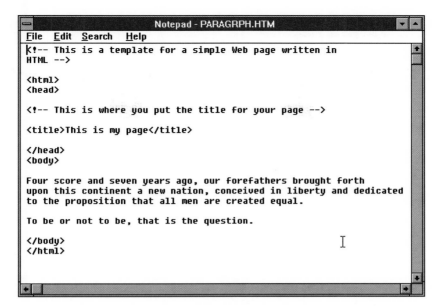

Figure 3

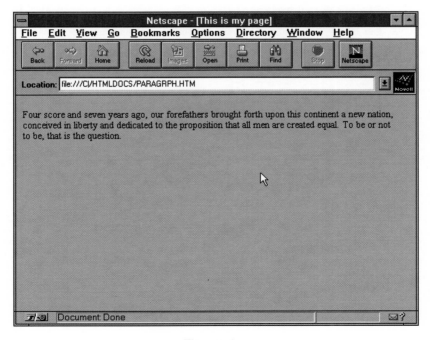

Figure 4

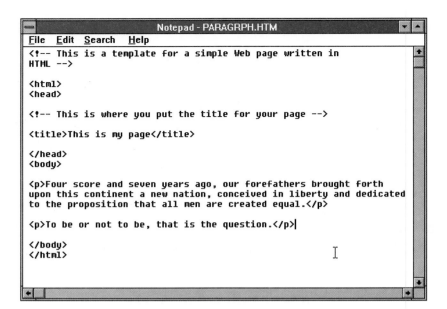

Figure 5

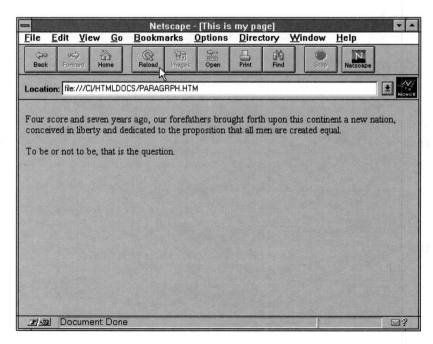

Figure 6

Your HTML document now looks like figure 5. Figure 6 shows how this looks when displayed with Netscape. This is probably closer to what you had in mind.

Interesting tidbit: the </p> tag, the tag we've used to mark where paragraphs end, doesn't actually do anything. Early versions of HTML didn't even have such a tag. It was added later so that the paragraph tag would work like other HTML tags. If you leave it out, the Web browser won't notice and the text will look exactly the same. Nonetheless, you should include it so that it will be clear where paragraphs begin and end. And it's possible that future Web browsers will require it.

THE <h>EADING TAGS

Many books, including this one, contain headings before certain paragraphs to tell you what those paragraphs are about. In fact, there's a heading right in front of the paragraph you are now reading. These headings help make the text clearer and the book easier to read by breaking it up into easily digested units. Headings are displayed in a different size from the rest of the text so that readers can tell them apart from ordinary text.

Headings are also common in Web pages and are recommended in any page longer than a few paragraphs. You can add headings to your HTML document by using the heading tags. In fact, there are actually six different heading tags, each ending with a number. The number indicates the level of the heading, from <h1> through <h6>. These headings are turned off using the numbered tags </h1> through </h6>.

The level of the heading determines how large it will appear on your Web page. The lower the level number, the larger the text. To see how this works, try typing these lines into the body of the HTML template we showed you earlier:

```
<h1>This is a first level heading.</h1>
<h2>This is a second level heading.</h2>
<h3>This is a third level heading.</h3>
<h4>This is a fourth level heading.</h4>
<h5>This is a fifth level heading.</h5>
<h6>This is a sixth level heading.</h6>
```

Your HTML document should now look like figure 7. When you view this with your Web browser, it should look something like figure 8.

LARGE AND SMALL TEXT

You can use the heading tags to do more than just create paragraph headings. You can use them to change the size of the text in the paragraphs on your Web page. Suppose you feel that the text on your page is too small. Then you can use a heading tag to make it larger, like this:

```
<h2><p>This is a large type paragraph. You could use
a paragraph like this to catch someone's attention or
for visually-impaired readers—or just because you like
the way it looks. And remember that there are six dif-
ferent heading tags, so you can get the exact size of
text that you want.</p></h2>
```

```
━                        Notepad - HEADINGS.HTM               ▼ ▲
 File   Edit   Search   Help
 <!-- This is a template for a simple Web page written in     ▲
 HTML -->

 <html>
 <head>

 <!-- This is where you put the title for your page -->

 <title>This is my page</title>

 </head>
 <body>

 <h1>This is a first level heading.</h1>
 <h2>This is a second level heading.</h2>
 <h3>This is a third level heading.</h3>
 <h4>This is a fourth level heading.</h4>
 <h5>This is a fifth level heading.</h5>
 <h6>This is a sixth level heading.</h6>

 </body>
 </html>                                           I
 |                                                            ▼
 ←                                                            →
```

Figure 7

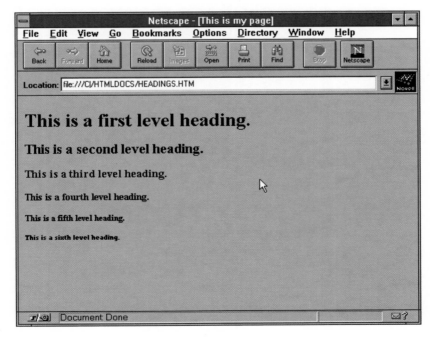

Figure 8

Type this into your template so that it looks like figure 9. Check out figure 10 to see how it appears in Netscape.

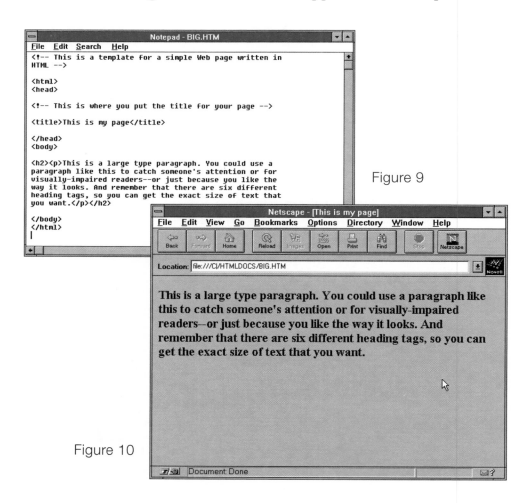

Figure 9

Figure 10

You can also use the heading tags to make your paragraph smaller by typing this into the body of your template:

\<h6\>\<p\>This is a small type paragraph. You could use a paragraph like this for information that you need to put into your page, but you don't want to get in the way of other text.\</p\>\</h6\>

Your HTML document should now look like figure 11. View this through your Web browser and it should look like the tiny text in figure 12.

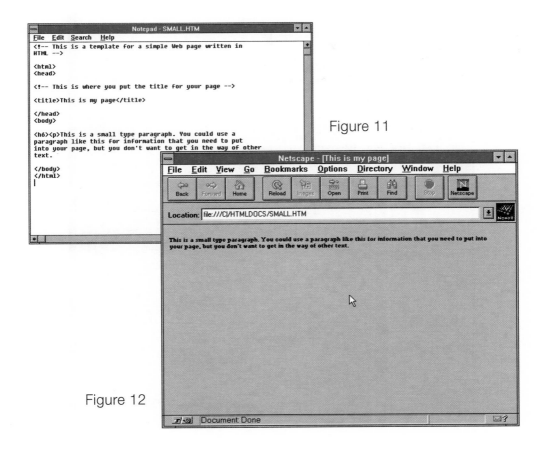

Figure 11

Figure 12

```
─                          Notepad - TYPE.HTM                      ▼ ▲
 File   Edit   Search   Help
 <!-- This is a template for a simple Web page written in  ▲
 HTML -->

 <html>
 <head>

 <!-- This is where you put the title for your page -->

 <title>This is my page</title>

 </head>
 <body>

 <p> A book can use several typefaces, such
 as <i>italicized text</i> and <b>boldfaced
 text</b>. So can a Web page.</p>

 </body>
 </html>

 |                                        I
                                                            ▼
 ←                                                          →
```

Figure 13

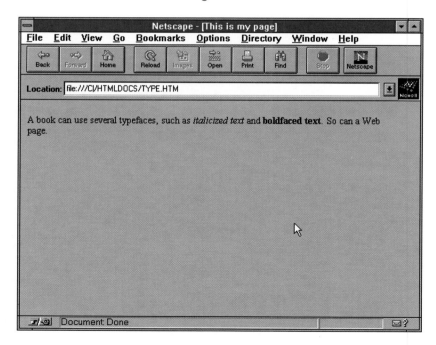

Figure 14

USING TYPEFACES

A book can use several typefaces, such as *italicized text* and **boldfaced text**. So can a Web page. Here's how we use these typefaces in the body of an HTML document:

```
<p> A book can use several typefaces, such as
<i>italicized text</i> and <b>boldfaced text</b>.
So can a Web page.</p>
```

Type this into your template so it looks like figure 13. To see the Web page version, go straight to figure 14.

As you've probably figured out from this example, the <i> and </i> tags turn italics on and off, and the <b> and </b> tags turn boldfacing on and off.

We can even create text that's italicized and boldfaced at the same time! Here's how:

```
<p>This is an example of <i><b> italicized
and boldfaced text </b></i>.
```

In your text editor, your HTML document now looks like figure 15, as shown on the next page. Under Netscape, it looks like what you see in figure 16. Notice that in the example above, the opening tags are ordered <i><b>. The order of the closing tags is reversed, </b></i>. This is important; you must always end the tag most recently opened before ending the tags preceding it.

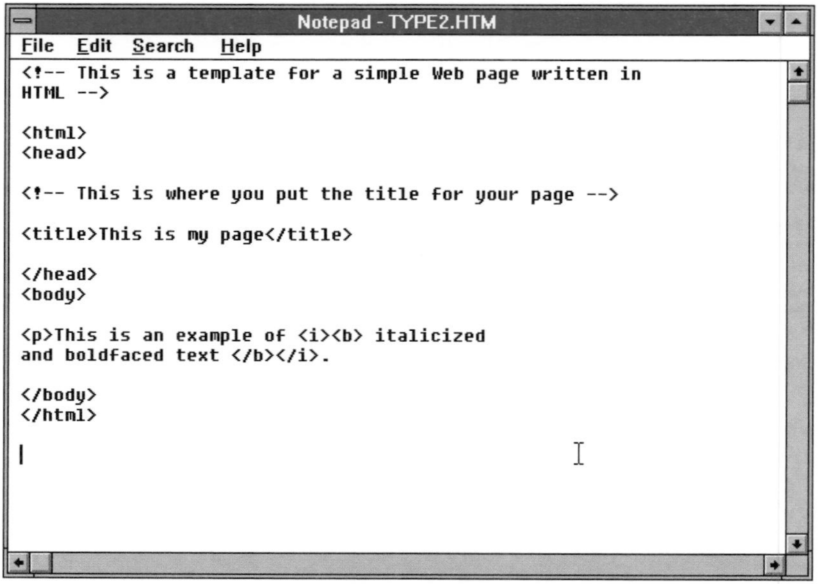

Notepad - TYPE2.HTM
File Edit Search Help
<!-- This is a template for a simple Web page written in HTML -->
<html>
<head>
<!-- This is where you put the title for your page -->
<title>This is my page</title>
</head>
<body>
<p>This is an example of <i><b> italicized
and boldfaced text </b></i>.
</body>
</html>

Figure 15

Netscape - [This is my page]
File Edit View Go Bookmarks Options Directory Window Help
Back
Forward
Home
Reload
Images
Open
Print
Find
Stop
Netscape
Location: file:///C|/HTMLDOCS/TYPE2.HTM
Novell
This is an example of italicized and boldfaced text .
Document: Done

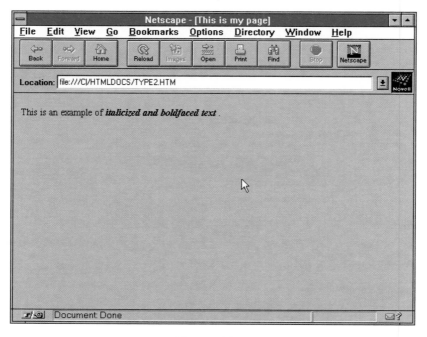

Figure 16

GO FOR IT!

At this point, you know enough about HTML text formatting to create a pretty slick looking Web page. So go for it! Run your text editor and Web browser and create a Web page of your own. Create several pages. And don't be afraid to experiment with HTML tags. The worst that can happen is that your Web browser will display your text in a way you never expected. And who knows? It may look better than the way you were planning to display the text in the first place!

There are two more elements that are essential to any Web page, though, and we'll be talking about those in the next chapter.

Anchors and Pictures

The people who created the World Wide Web imagined it as being one big *hypertext* document. In some ways, a hypertext document is like a giant electronic book that exists on computers, with different parts of the book connected to other parts using hyperlinks. When you click on a hyperlink with your mouse pointer, it takes you to another part of the book. For instance, if you're reading a part of the book that concerns Africa, you might see a hyperlink about lions. When you click on this hyperlink, you'll go to a different part of the book that talks about lions in greater detail.

In fact, the Web is made up of millions of hypertext documents that are linked together. The hypertext documents that make up the World Wide Web are stored on many thousands of computers worldwide and consist of many, many millions of words. It covers subjects as diverse as computers and comic books, politics and poetry, space travel and auto repair. We get from one of these subjects to another via hyperlinks. Hyperlinks commonly take the form of colored, underlined words or phrases. When you move your mouse cursor over a hyperlink, the arrow changes into a pointing hand, and clicking on the mouse button will activate the link.

Let's add some hyperlinks to our Web pages. To do this, we'll use HTML anchors.

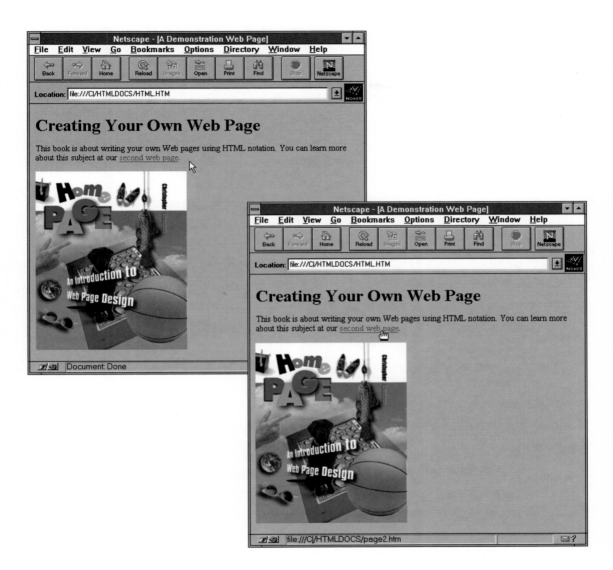

As you move the mouse cursor over a hyperlink, it changes
from an arrow (top) into a pointing hand (bottom).

THE <a>NCHOR TAG

A typical anchor tag looks like this:

<a href="destination">text of hyperlink</a>

This is a complicated tag, so we'll study it in some detail. The first letter "a" simply tells us that this is an anchor. The "href" tells us that it's a hypertext link. This means that when we click on it, we'll go to a different location on the Web. (We'll look at a different type of anchor in a moment.)

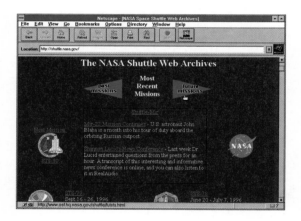

Figure 17

The "destination" is the place that we'll be going to when we click on that hyperlink. This destination can be any of several things. For instance, it can be a completely different place on the Web, in which case you would put the address, or *URL* (Uniform Resource Locator), for that place between the quotation marks in the anchor tag. Suppose you're a big fan of NASA's Space Shuttle site on the Web (pictured in figure 17) and want to include a link to it from your Web page. The address of the Space Shuttle site is **http://shuttle.nasa.gov**. So you could begin the anchor this way:

<a href="http://shuttle.nasa.gov">

The "text of the hyperlink" is what you want the hyper-link to say on your page. This is the actual text that the user will click on to follow the link. For instance, the paragraph about the Space Shuttle site might read:

<p>One of my favorite sites on the World Wide
Web is NASA's site about the Space Shuttle.
To go to that site, just click
<a href="http://shuttle.nasa.gov">here</a>.</p>

If you type this into the body of your template, your HTML document will look like figure 18. Take a look at this paragraph in Netscape and you'll see something like the image in figure 19. Notice that the word "here" is in a dif-

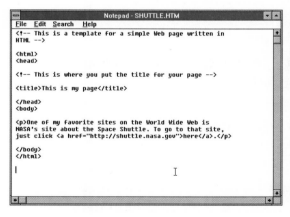

Figure 18

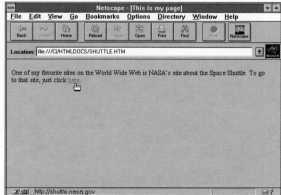

Figure 19

ferent color from
the rest of the text
and is underlined.
This tells you that
it's a hyperlink.
Click on it and
you'll go to the
Space Shuttle site.
(Note that you
need to have a
connection to the
World Wide Web
in order to go
there. If you're

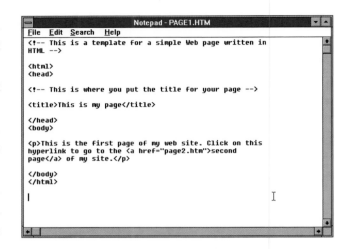

Figure 20

running your Web browser offline when you click on this
hyperlink, you'll just get an error message. Don't let it
stop you from experimenting with anchors.)

CREATING A WEB SITE

You can also use hyperlinks to jump between two or more
pages that you've created yourself. When you create more
than one Web page and link them together, you've created
a full-fledged *Web site*. So what are we waiting for? Let's create a site!

Make two copies of the HTML template we created
earlier. Name the first one **page1.htm** and the second one
page2.htm. Put them in the same place on your hard disk,
that is, on the same drive and in the same directory. (If you

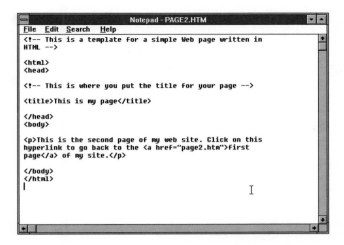

Figure 21

don't know about drives and directories, ask a friend, parent, or teacher who knows about computers.)

Now use your text editor to put the following text in the body of the document that you have named **page1.htm**:

<p>This is the first page of my web site. Click on this hyperlink to go to the <a href ="page2.htm">second page</a> of my site.</p>

The HTML document named **page1.htm** should now look like figure 20. Type this text into the body of the document named **page2.htm**:

<p>This is the second page of my web site. Click on this hyperlink to go back to the <a href="page2.htm">first page</a> of my site.</p>

Figure 21 shows the new **page2.htm**. If you look at these two pages with your Web browser, they should look like figures 22 and 23. You'll notice that the words "second page" are now a hyperlink in the file **page1.htm**, and the words "first page" are now a hyperlink in the file **page2.htm**.

But the most important thing about these files is that if you click on either of these hyperlinks your Web browser will automatically take you from one page to the other. You've created a Web site!

Of course, there's no reason you have to restrict your Web site to only two pages. You can add a third page or another thirty. And you can include hyperlinks that will allow you to jump between these pages at the click of a mouse!

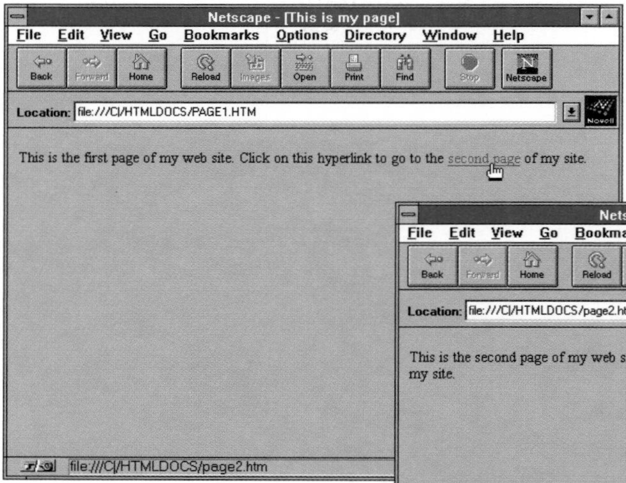

Figure 22

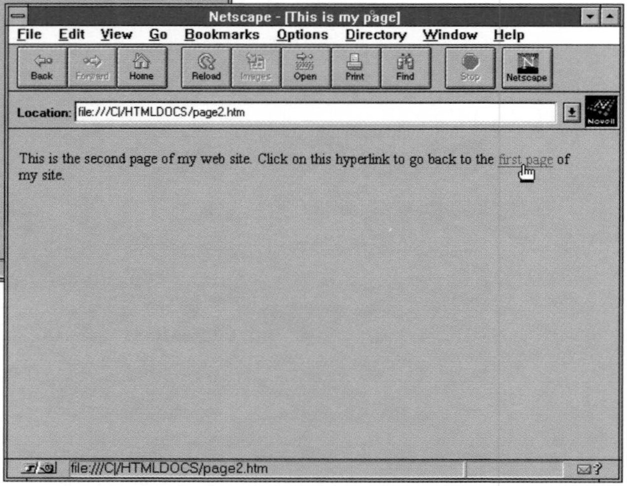

Figure 23

TARGETS WITHIN A PAGE

You can even use hyperlinks to jump to another place in the same page. This is especially useful if you've created a very long page and want to be able to jump to different parts quickly. The place in the page that you jump to is called a *target*. You can create a target using an anchor tag. This is a slightly different use of the anchor tag than we described earlier, and it looks like this:

```
<a name="target">target text</a>
```

The "target" in the anchor above is the name of the target. You'll use this name later to create a hyperlink that jumps to this location. The target text is the text that will actually appear in your Web page at the location of the target. The name of the target and the target text can be the same, but they don't have to be.

To jump to this target, you can create a hyperlink elsewhere in your page that looks like this:

```
<a href="#target">hyperlink text</a>
```

The destination of this type of hyperlink is the name of the anchor with a number sign (#) in front of it, in this case "#target."

Here's an example of a simple HTML body with a hypertext link that jumps to a target in the same page:

```
<p>Later on, I'll show you how to do a magic trick. If you want to read about it now, click <a href="#trick">here</a>.</p>
```


<p>Okay, <a name="trick">here's</a> that magic trick I promised you.</p>

Type this into the body of your template so it looks like figure 24. You'll notice that we've introduced a new formatting tag here. The <br> tag ends (or breaks) the previous line. (There's no </br> tag.) Typing two consecutive <br> tags puts a blank line in your page. We've used the <br> tag here so that the first and second paragraphs don't appear on the screen together. Otherwise it wouldn't be much of a trick when you click on the hyperlink "here" and go automatically to the next paragraph.

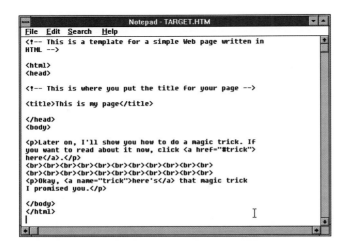

Figure 24

You can use hyperlinks to go to targets in the middle of other pages, too. Just use the anchor tag to create a target the way we showed you a moment ago. In another page, create a hyperlink like this:

<a href="filename#target">hyperlink text</a>

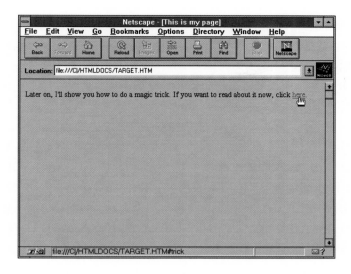

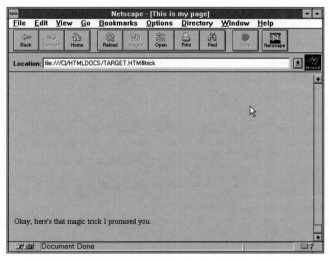

The HTML document shown in figure 24 creates this Web page. Clicking on the hyperlink near the top of this page (top) allows you to jump to a target at the bottom of the page (bottom).

In this example, "filename" is the name of the file, such as **mypage.htm**, that contains the target you created.

That should be enough information to get you started with hyperlinks, but what about pictures?

ADDING PICTURES TO YOUR PAGE

Before you can add a picture to your Web page, you must have a picture to add. This may seem obvious, but creating or finding a picture can often be the hardest part of creating a Web page. However, it's also one of the most important parts, since adding pictures to your Web page will make it look more attractive and professional.

One way to create pictures is to draw them yourself. There are plenty of computer programs that will help you do this. You can also buy pictures. At your local software store, you can find packages of clip art—pictures you purchase that you can put into your Web page. (Make sure the clip art is intended for a Web page, though, and not for a desktop publishing program, since these two types of pictures may be stored on your disk in very different ways.) Or you can download packages of clip art from the Web itself.

GRAPHICS FILE FORMATS

A picture to be included in a Web page must be stored in the correct way on your hard disk. The way in which a picture is stored is referred to as a *graphics file format*. There are many different graphics file formats, but only two of them can be used with a Web browser. These two formats are called GIF (pronounced "giff" or "jiff") and JPEG (pronounced "jay peg").

Figure 25

You can tell if a picture is stored in one of these formats because the name of the file containing the picture on your disk will usually end with either **.gif** or **.jpg**. If you have a picture you want to use that is not in a compatible format, many programs available on the Web can help you convert your picture to a GIF or JPEG file.

Once you have a picture that's stored in one of these formats, you can include it in your Web page using the <img src> tag, which looks like this:

<img src="filename">

For instance, we have a picture called **schubert.gif** (shown in figure 25). We can put this picture into our Web page by typing this into the body of the template:

<body>

<p>My friend David has a beagle named Schubert. This is a picture of Schubert.</p>

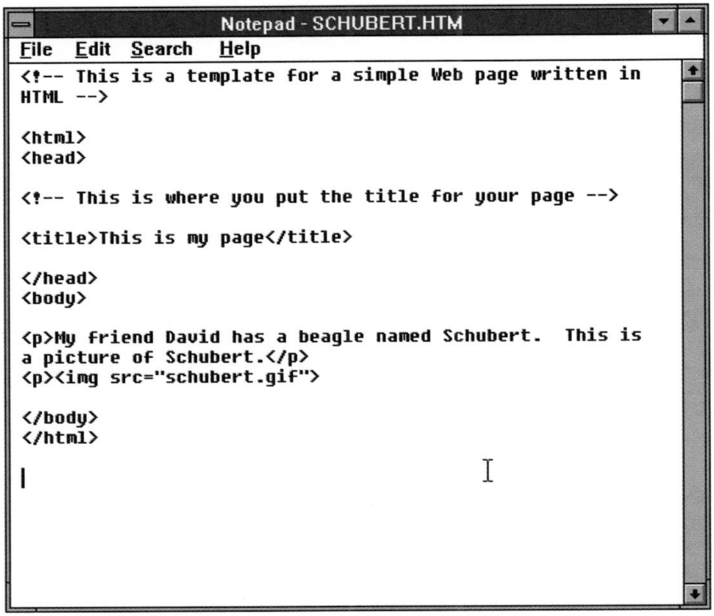

Notepad - SCHUBERT.HTM
File Edit Search Help
<!-- This is a template for a simple Web page written in
HTML -->
<html>
<head>
<!-- This is where you put the title for your page -->
<title>This is my page</title>
</head>
<body>
<p>My friend David has a beagle named Schubert. This is
a picture of Schubert.</p>
<p><img src="schubert.gif">
</body>
</html>

Figure 26

Netscape - [This is my page]
File Edit View Go Bookmarks Options Directory Window Help
Back
Forward
Home
Reload
Images
Open
Print
Find
Stop
Netscape
Location: file:///C|/HTMLDOCS/SCHUBERT.HTM
My friend David has a beagle named Schubert. This is a picture of Schubert.
Document: Done

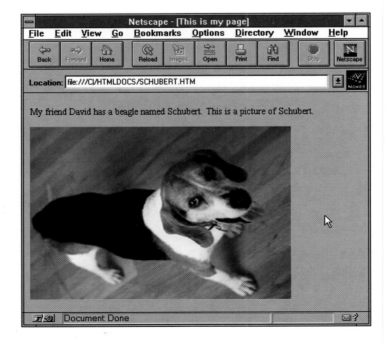

Figure 27

```
<p><img src="schubert.gif">

</body>
```

The <p>aragraph tag in front of the <img src> tag assures us that the picture will appear on a new line and not right after the most recent text. The new HTML document looks like figure 26. If we view this page with Netscape, it looks like figure 27.

If you have some pictures that are in either the GIF or JPEG format, try putting them in the same directory as your HTML files. Then put the pictures into your Web pages using <img src>. Once again, don't be afraid to experiment. The results will be worth it!

GO FOR IT (AGAIN)

That's all the space we have in this book to tell you about creating your own Web pages. But it's enough to get you started. In fact, you can create some truly excellent Web pages using just the information in this book and a little imagination.

However, there are other things that can be done with HTML. And the best place to learn about them is on the World Wide Web itself. Fire up your connection to the Web, run your browser and use a *search engine* or a *Web index* such as Yahoo (at **http://www.yahoo.com**) to find all the references you can to HTML. You'll discover that there's plenty of information on the Web about writing HTML documents. And,

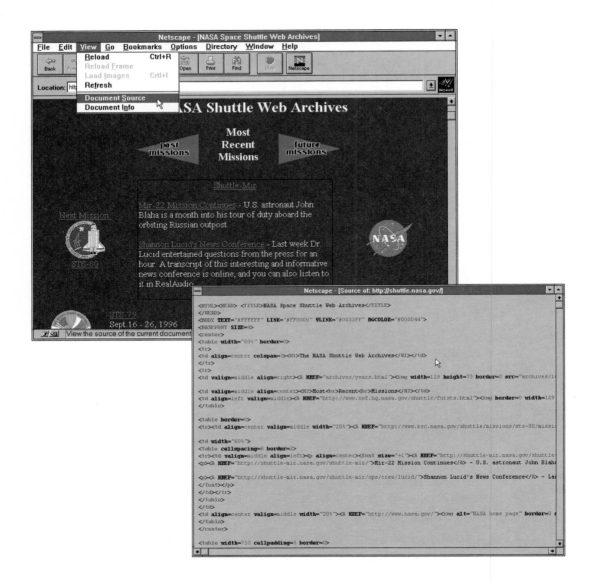

In Netscape, you can view the source of this Space Shuttle page by clicking on Document Source under the View menu (top). This brings you a window containing the HTML document for this page (bottom).

if this isn't enough, go to your local bookstore or library and look for some more advanced books on the subject.

Another excellent way to learn additional HTML tags is to examine the source of actual Web pages. If, while browsing the Web with Netscape, you encounter a page that you like, you can study the HTML document behind it by clicking on the View menu and selecting Document Source. Netscape will display a window containing the HTML document for that page.

You'll notice that we haven't said anything in this book about how to get your Web pages on the Web itself. There's a reason for this. The way in which you do this depends on where you plan to put your page.

If you belong to an online service such as America Online or CompuServe, they'll probably give you some free space on the Web to put up your page. Check with those services to find out how to upload your HTML documents to the Web.

If you belong to a different *Internet service provider,* they may rent you space for your Web page for a few dollars a month. Check with your Internet provider for details. Some places on the Web will even let you put up your own pages for free. But you'll have to find these on your own.

No matter how you get your page on the Web, though, you'll find that the information in this book on writing HTML documents will serve you well. Good luck with your page!

Glossary

anchor – a tag used to put a hyperlink or target in a Web page.

body – the main part of an HTML document, which contains all the text, pictures, and hyperlinks that will appear in the Web page.

comment tags – the <!-- and --> tags; used in an HTML document to include a note that will not appear in the Web page.

data files – the form in which information, including computer programs, is stored on your computer's disk drive(s).

download – to transfer programs and other files from the Internet to your computer's hard drive or to a diskette.

files – see *data files*.

graphics file format – the way in which an image is stored on a disk.

hard drive – a permanent, magnetic disk inside your computer that stores computer programs and other types of information so that you can access them easily.

header – part of a HTML document where you can specify the title of the Web page.

heading – words in a Web page that are in a different size from the rest of the text.

HTML – short for HyperText Markup Language, this is the form in which Web pages are written.

hyperlink – a word or image representing a connection between one part of the World Wide Web and another part.

hypertext – text containing hyperlinks to other documents

HyperText Markup Language – see *HTML*.

image tag – a tag used to place and image in a Web page.

Internet – a group of computers around the world that are connected together in such a way that each can send information to the others.

Internet service provider – a company that provides Internet service to individuals, businesses, and institutions.

paragraph tags – the <p> and </p> tags; used to indicate where paragraphs begin and end.

search engines – computer programs on the Web that allow you to search for pages containing words that you specify.

source – the HTML document that creates a Web page.

tag – letters or words between angle brackets that activate the features of HTML.

target – a type of anchor that lets you designate a specific location within a Web page for a hyperlink to jump to.

template – a simple HTML document used as a pattern to create other Web pages.

text editor – a program used for creating and editing text files.

text file – a type of computer file that contains words, numbers, and symbols.

URL – short for Uniform Resource Locator, this is the "address" of a Web page and is how your Web browser finds a page on the Web.

Web browser – a program that reads files written in HTML and displays them on your computer screen with formatted text and pictures.

Web index – a site on the Web that consists mostly of hyperlinks to other sites.

Web page – an HTML file when it's viewed using a Web browser.

Web site – a collection of Web pages stored on an Internet computer where they can be read by your Web browser.

World Wide Web – a large collection of files on the Internet that are connected by hyperlinks. The information can be accessed using a computer and a Web browser.

For Further Reading

Horton, William. *The Web Page Design Cookbook: All the Ingredients You Need to Create 5-star Web Pages.* New York: Wiley, 1996.

McFedries, Paul. *The Complete Idiot's Guide to Creating an HTML Web Page.* Indianapolis: Que, 1996.

Musciano, Chuck and Bill Kennedy. *HTML, the Definitive Guide.* Sebastopol, CA: O'Reilly & Associates,1996.

Niederst, Jennifer with Edie Freedman. *Designing for the Web: Getting Started in a New Medium.* Sebastopol, CA: O'Reilly & Associates, 1996.

Tittel, Ed and Steve James. *HTML for Dummies.* Foster City, CA: IDG Books, 1996.

Smith, Bud and Arthur Bebak. *Creating Web Pages for Dummies.* Foster City, CA: IDG Books, 1996.

Index

About the Author

Noted science writer Christopher Lampton has written more than seventy-five books on subjects such as astronomy, computers, genetic engineering, meteorology, and the environment. He is the author of the best-selling *Flights of Fantasy*, about advanced computer game programming. In addition to his nonfiction, he has written several science fiction novels, as well as adventure novels for young adults. Mr. Lampton holds a degree in broadcast communications, and he makes his home in Gaithersburg, Maryland.